ScottForesman

D'Nealian® Handwriting

Third Edition

Book 1

Author
Donald Neal Thurber

ScottForesman

Editorial Offices: Glenview, Illinois
Regional Offices: Sunnyvale, California • Tucker, Georgia
Glenview, Illinois • Oakland, New Jersey • Dallas, Texas

Acknowledgments

Text
Page 73: Text and art from *"Pardon?" Said the Giraffe* by Colin West. Copyright © 1986 by Colin West. Reprinted by permission of HarperCollins Publishers and Walker Books Limited.
Page 141: From *Eat Up, Gemma* written by Sarah Hayes. Illustrated by Jan Ormerod. Text copyright © 1988 by Sarah Hayes. Illustrations copyright © 1988 by Jan Ormerod. Published by Lothrop, Lee & Shepard Books, a Division of William Morrow & Company, Inc. Reprinted by permission of William Morrow and Company, Inc. and Walker Books Limited.

Illustrations
Leslie Bowman: 54; Cindy Brodie 16, 58, 111, 116, 117, 119, 120; Nan Brooks 27, 87; Rondi Collette 93, 94, 95, 96, 97, 99, 100; Laura D'Argo 34, 39, 46, 138; Judith dufour-Love 12, 19, 64; Creston Ely 26, 37, 51; Marla Frazee 15; Lydia Halvorsen 65; Linda Hawkins 42; Gary Hoover 18, 29, 30, 38, 43, 76, 91, 92, 131; Deb Morse 22, 23, 56, 59, 63; Susan Nethery 21, 24, 60, 69, 133, 134; Cheryl Kirk-Noll 17; Sharron O'Neil 13, 102, 103, 106, 109; Stella Ormai 35, 45, 47, 55, 57, 67; Jan Palmer 121, 122, 123, 124, 126, 129, 130; Robert Pasternak 68; Gary Phillips 112, 113, 114, 115, 119; Gail Roth 48; Judy Sakaguchi 86; Cindy Salans-Rosenheim 105, 107, 109; Carol Schwartz 44, 52, 101, 104, 109, 110; Jeff Severn 20, 41, 71, 72, 89, 140; Bob Shein 11, 25, 32; Lena Shiffman 36, 90; Georgia Shola 132; Carol Stutz 74, 142; Susan Swan 49, 135; Peggy Tagel 33, 37, 38 (wagon, chest, and train); Titus Tomescu 15, 40; Jenny Vainisi 53, 61, 66; Darcy Whitehead 3, 4, 5, 31 33, 77, 85; Jeannie Winston 125, 127, 129

Photographs
H. Armstrong Roberts 132

Staff Credits
Editorial: Marianne Hiland, Gerry Murphy-Ferguson, Delores Nemo, and Bonnie Turell
Design: Paula Meyers
Production: Barbara Albright and Maryann Lewis
Marketing: Sue Cowden and Kristine Stanczak

D'Nealian® Handwriting is a registered trademark of Donald Neal Thurber.

ISBN: 0-673-28530-8
Copyright © 1993
Scott, Foresman and Company, Glenview, Illinois
All Rights Reserved. Printed in the United States of America.

36 37 38 39 40 -V064- 12 11 10 09 08

Contents

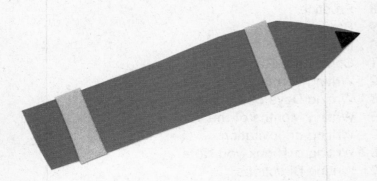

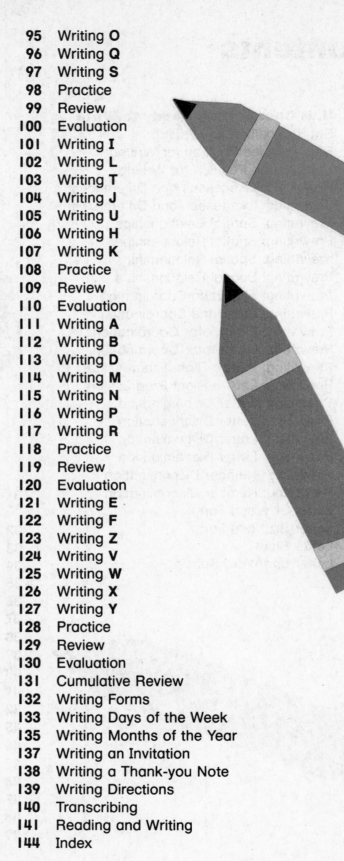

Unit One
Getting Ready to Write

Sitting Position for Writing

Sit tall.
Put both feet on the floor.

Left-handed

Right-handed

Children position themselves comfortably for writing

Right-handed Position for Writing

Slant your paper as shown
in the picture.

Hold it with your left hand.

Hold your pencil lightly between
your fingers.

Study the picture.

Children practice the proper position of
their papers and pencils for good writing.

Left-handed Position for Writing

Slant your paper as shown in the picture.

Hold it with your right hand.

Hold your pencil lightly between your fingers.

Study the picture.

8　Left-handed Position for Writing

Children practice the proper position of their papers and pencils for good writing.

Circle the pictures.

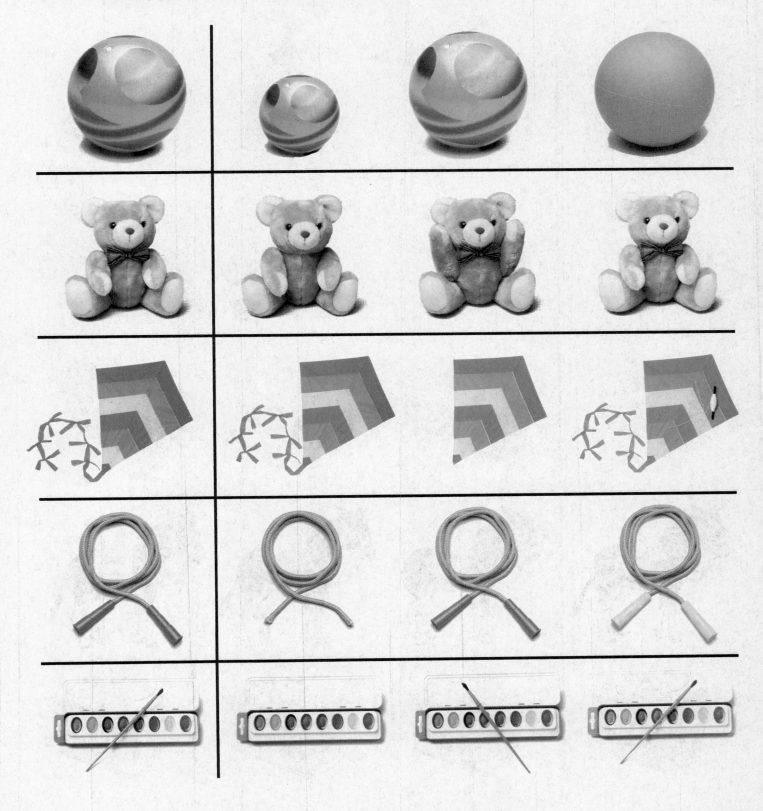

Prewriting: Likenesses and Differences   **9**

Children circle the picture that matches the first one in each row.

Circle the pictures.

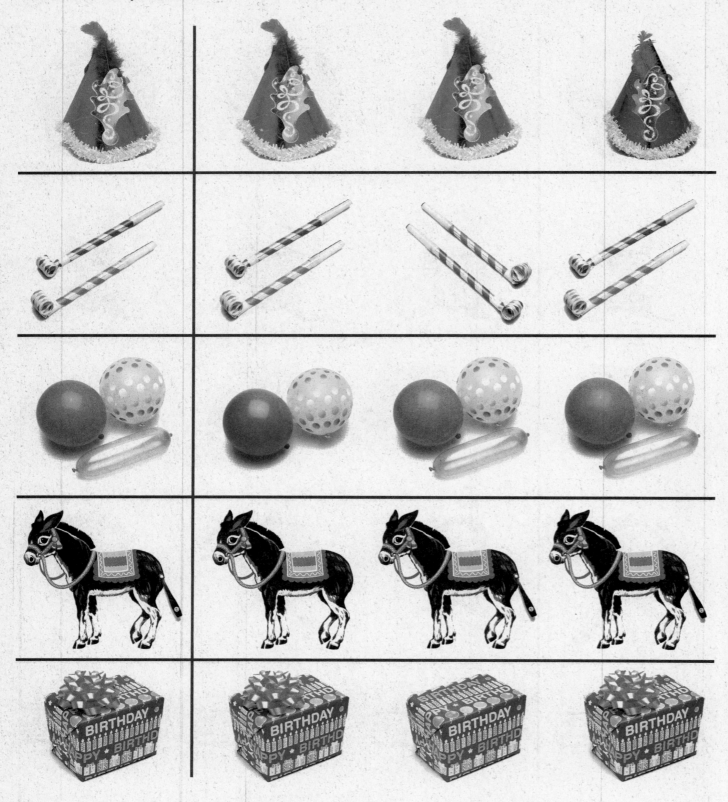

10   Prewriting: Likenesses and Differences

Children circle the picture that is different in each row.

Draw and color.

Children draw and color a window with blue curtains on the **top** floor, a window with yellow curtains on the **middle** floor, and a window with green curtains on the **bottom** floor.

Draw and color.

12 Prewriting: Spatial Relationships
Children draw and color a footpath **around** the picture of the art fair.

Mark the pictures.

Children circle each animal **above** the water
and underline each animal **below** the water.

Mark the pictures.

Prewriting: Spatial Relationships

Children circle each puppet **over** the table and underline each child **under** it.

Draw the lines.

Children locate the arrows and the starting dots. Then
they draw lines within the paths to the dots at the end.

Draw a line.

16   Prewriting: Eye-Hand Coordination

Children locate the arrow and the starting dot. Then
they draw a line within the path to the dot at the end.

Trace the tools.
Color.

Children trace and color the tools for the garden.

Trace and color.
Cut and paste.

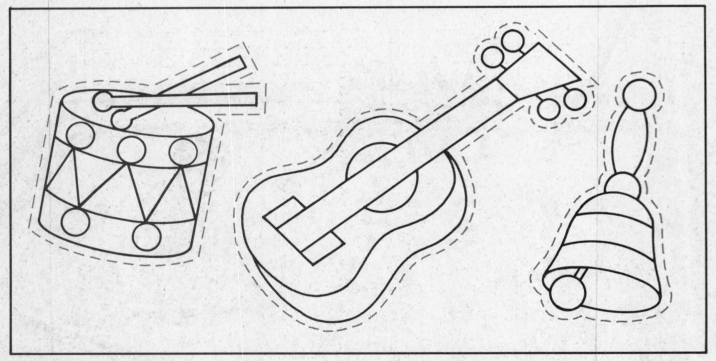

Prewriting: Fine Motor Coordination

Children color and trace the instruments at the bottom of the page.
Then they cut out the instruments and paste them in the music chest.

Draw the lines.

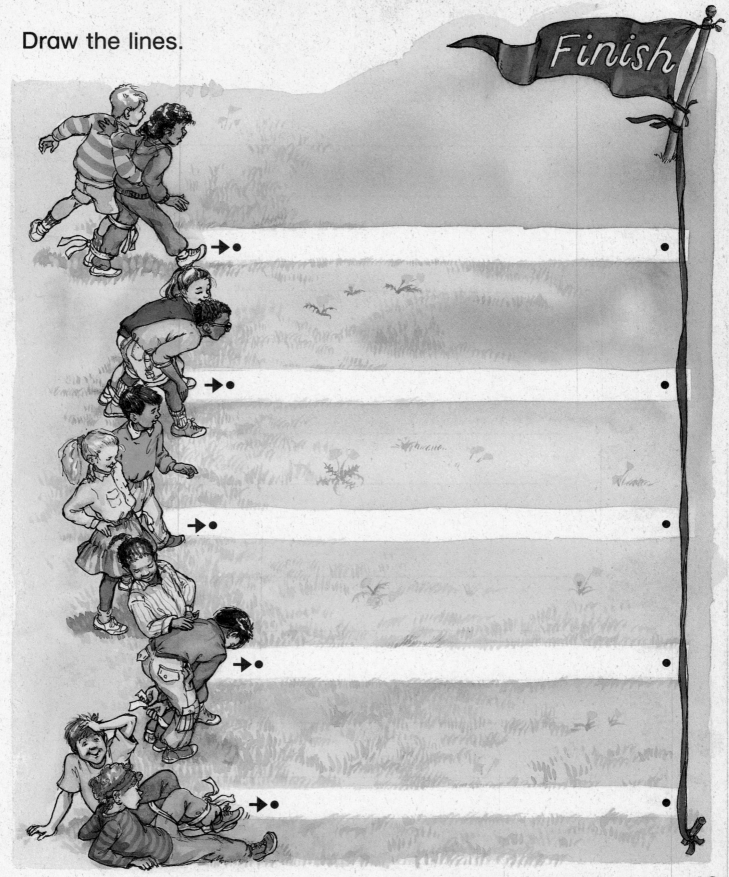

Children locate the arrows and the starting dots. Then they draw lines within the paths to the dots at the end.

Draw the lines.

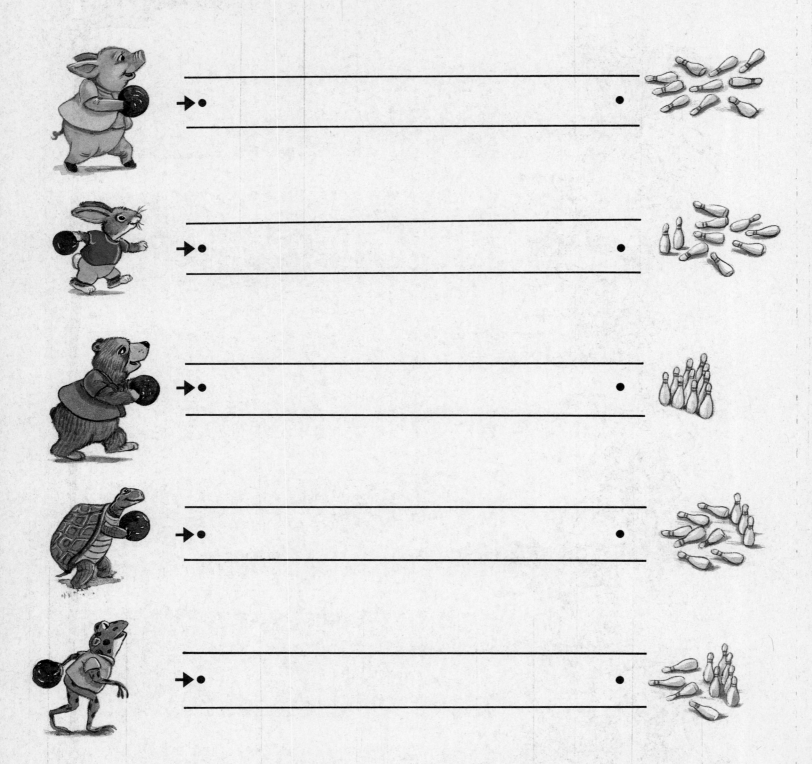

20   Prewriting: Left-to-Right Progression

Children locate the arrows and the starting dots. Then
they draw lines within the paths to the dots at the end.

Match.
Circle the letters.

a | l r o a

y | n u y c

h | h m t w

p | q p b g

j | i j k d

Children circle the letter that matches the first one in each row.

Match.
Circle the letters.

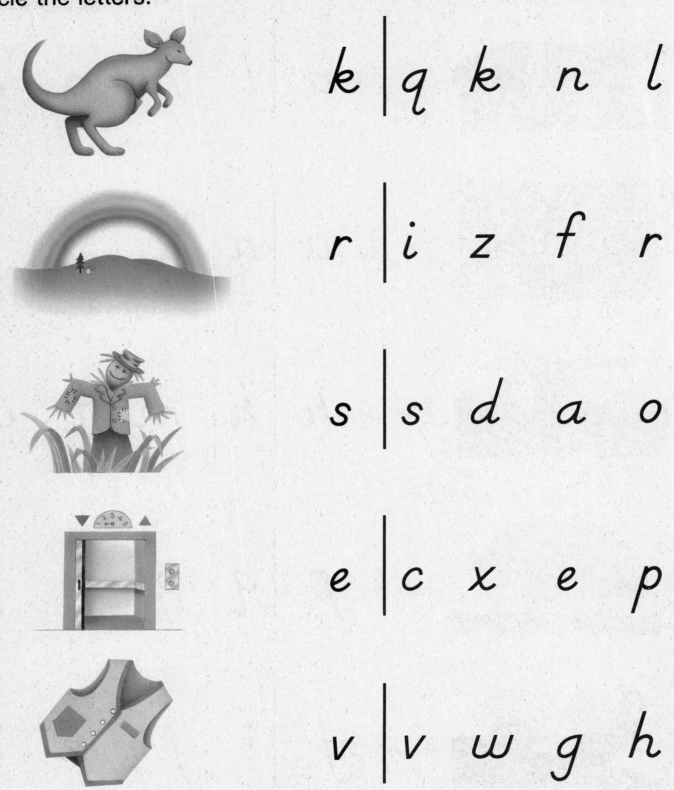

k	q	k	n	l
r	i	z	f	r
s	s	d	a	o
e	c	x	e	p
v	v	w	g	h

Children circle the letter that matches the first one in each row.

Match.
Circle the letters.

I	T I J K
B	A Z B P
D	D R O S
C	Q V C Y
W	E U M W

Children circle the letter that matches the first one in each row.

Match.
Circle the letters.

T | L N T E

M | M I J P

O | D O U B

G | W G C X

Z | H R A Z

Prewriting: Letter Discrimination
Children circle the letter that matches the first one in each row.

Draw and color.

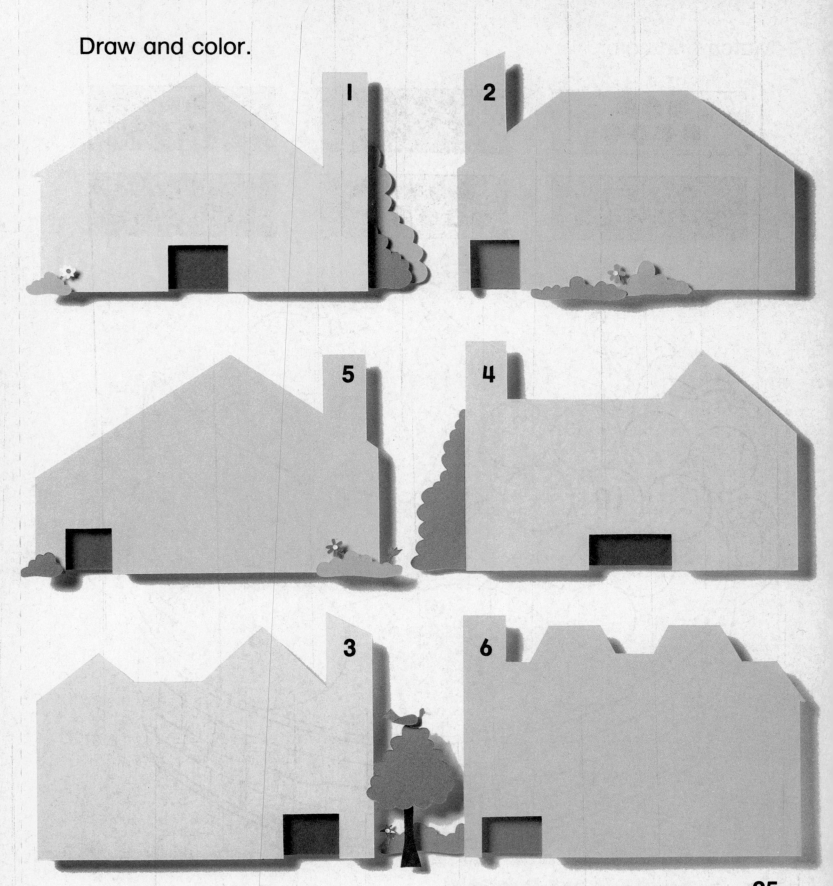

Children draw and color a specific number of windows
in each picture to represent the number shown.

Match and color.

Prewriting: Number Discrimination

Children match the number of dots in each box with
each number in the fruit basket and color the picture.

Animals can help you remember the size of letters.

A   is tall.

These letters are tall.

b d f h k l t

A   is small.

These letters are small.

a c e i m n o

r s u v w x z

A   has a tail that falls.

These letters fall.

g j p q y

Children compare the size of animals to
the relative size of lower-case letters.

Look at the size of each letter.
Draw the correct animal to match each group.

b d f h
k l t

a c e i m
n o r s u
v w x z

g j p q y

Letter Size and Form

Children draw a picture of a giraffe to represent tall letters, a dog
to represent small letters, and a cat to represent descender letters.

Letters should slant the same way.
Color the kites that can fly.

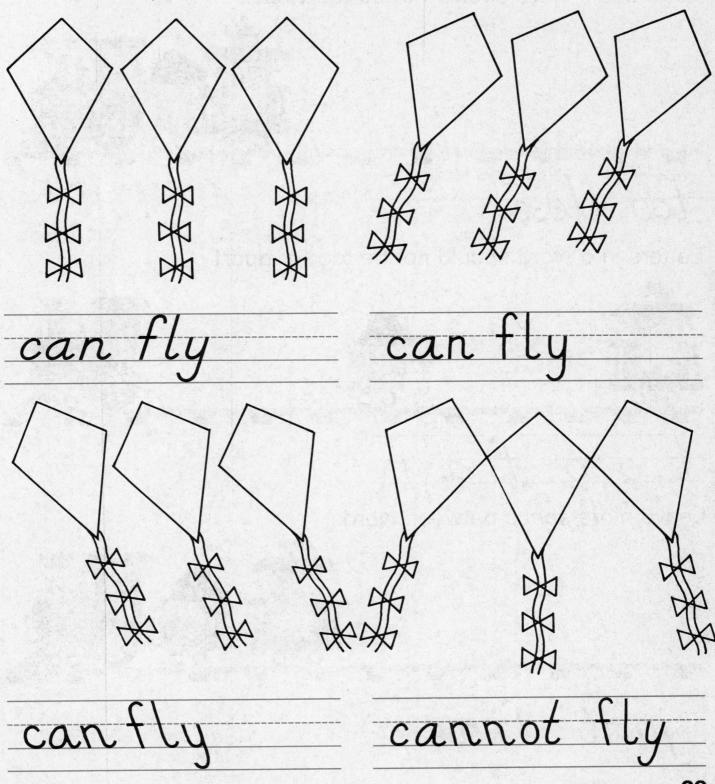

can fly

can fly

can fly

cannot fly

Children compare the slant of each group of kites to the letters in each group.
Then they color each group of kites that is slanted in the same direction.

You need to space letters and words.

Letters in a word should not be too close.

too close

Letters in a word should not be too far apart.

t o o f a r

Leave more space between words.

just fine

30   Letter and Word Spacing
Children compare correct and incorrect letter and word spacing.

Unit Two

Writing Lower-case Letters

There are many ways to write the same letter.
Circle each **p.**
Draw a line under each **o.**
Draw a box around each **e.**

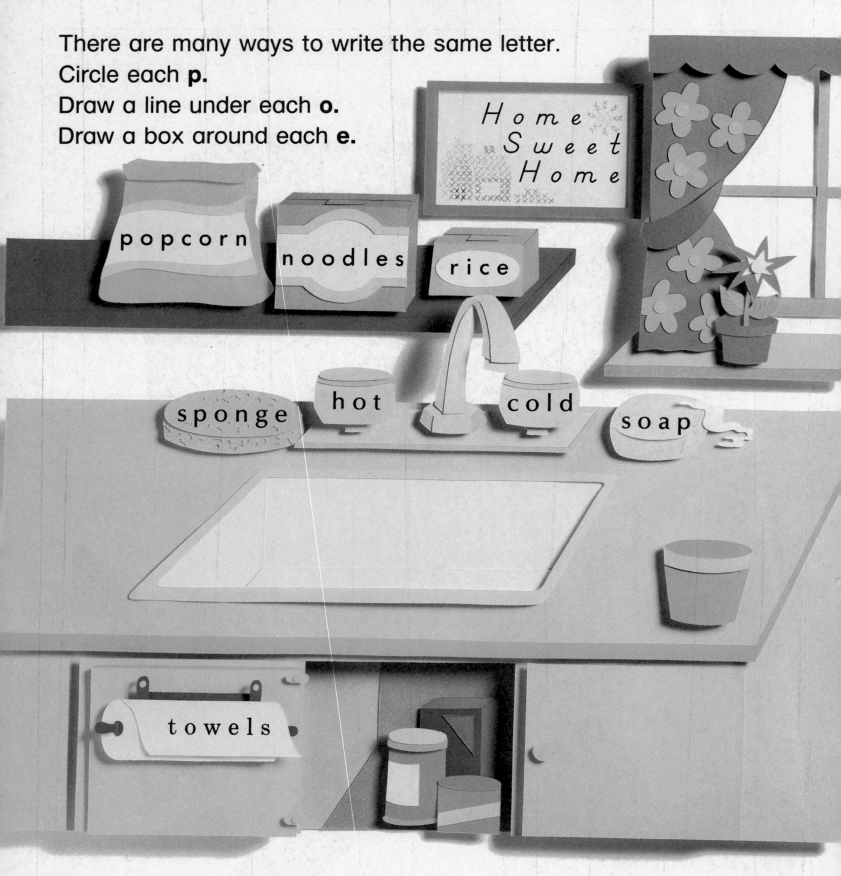

Home
Sweet
Home

popcorn

noodles

rice

sponge

hot

cold

soap

towels

Children compare the same letters in different type styles. Then they
circle each **p**, underline each **o**, and draw a box around each **e.**

apple

ant

a

a

My Words

Children trace and write the letter **a** and the word **a**.

d

door

dog

d d d d • • d

My Words

add

add

dad

dad

Children trace and write the letter **d** and the words **add** and **dad**.

o

otter

octopus

odd

odd

My Words

Children trace and write the letter **o** and the word **odd**.

g

girl

gift

g *g* *g* *g*

My Words

dog

dog

good

good

Children trace and write the letter **g** and the words **dog** and **good**.

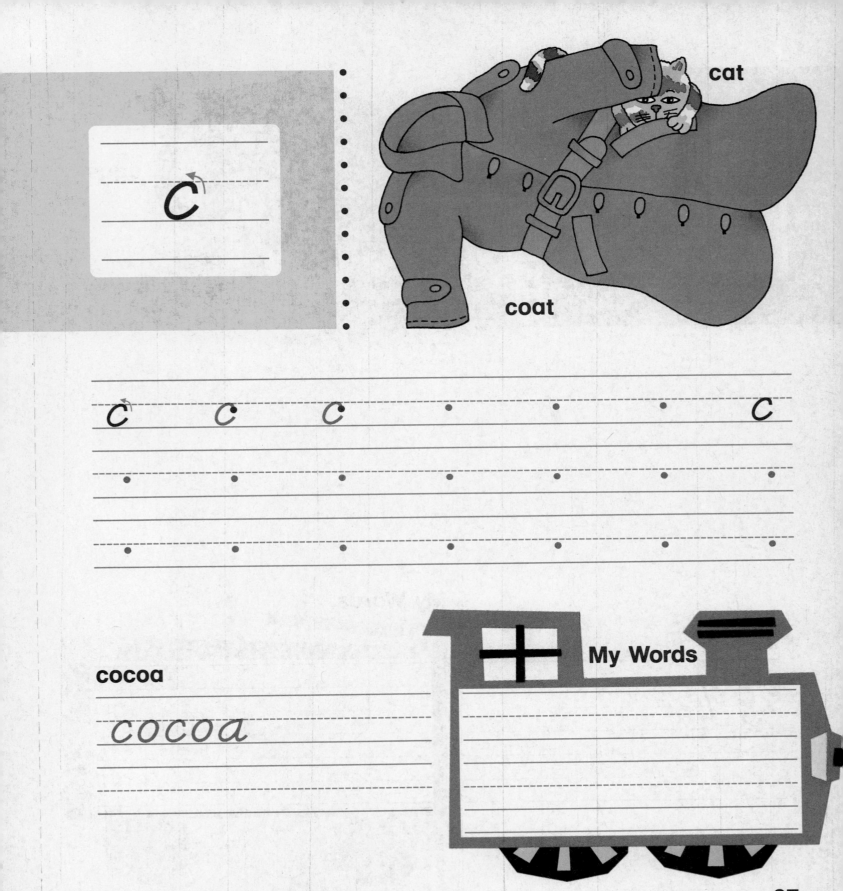

cat

coat

C

c   c   c   •   •   •   c

cocoa

cocoa

My Words

Children trace and write the letter **c** and the word **cocoa**.

elephant

eggs

e

e   e   e   •   •   •   e

egg

egg

My Words

Children trace and write the letter **e** and the word **egg**.

S

sun

sandbox

s s s • • • s

My Words

sea

sea

see

see

Children trace and write the letter s and the words **sea** and **see**.

Practice

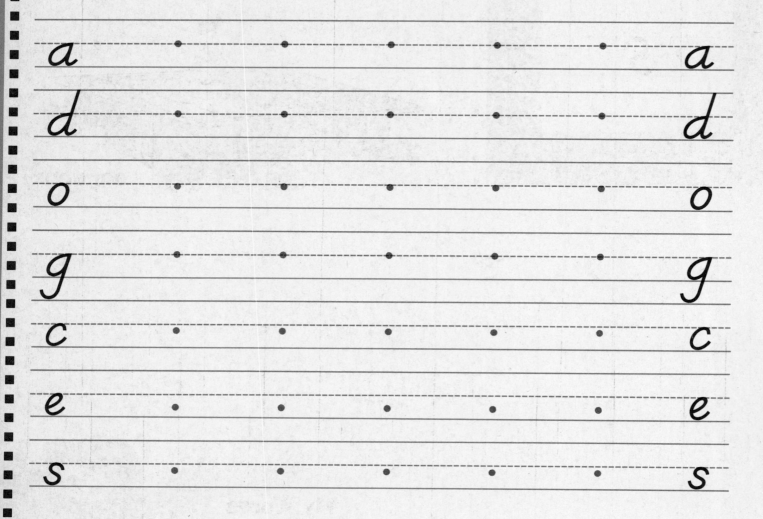

a a

d d

o o

g g

c c

e e

s s

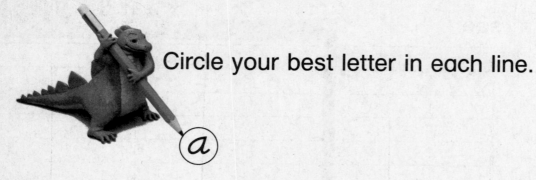

Circle your best letter in each line.

$ⓐ$

Children write the letters **a, d, o, g, c, e,** and **s.**

Review

dog

dog

dogs

dogs

cage

cage

cages

cages

goose

goose

geese

geese

seed

seed

seeds

seeds

Children trace and write words with the letters **a**, **d**, **o**, **g**, **c**, **e**, and **s**.

Evaluation

Remember: Close the letters **a**, **d**, **o**, and **g**.

dad

dad

cage

cage

a goose

a goose

good dogs

good dogs

Check Your Handwriting
Did you close the letters **a**, **d**, **o**, and **g**?

Yes   No

☐   ☐

42   Evaluation

Children trace and write words and phrases
with the letters **a**, **d**, **o**, **g**, **c**, **e**, and **s**.

f

2→ f

fish

fence

f   f   f   .   .   .   f

My Words

off

off

feed

feed

Writing **f**   **43**

Children trace and write the letter **f** and the words **off** and **feed**.

boy

ball

base

base

bag

bag

My Words

Children trace and write the letter **b** and the words **base** and **bag**.

l

lake

lion

l l l ⋯ *l*

leaf

leaf

fall

fall

My Words

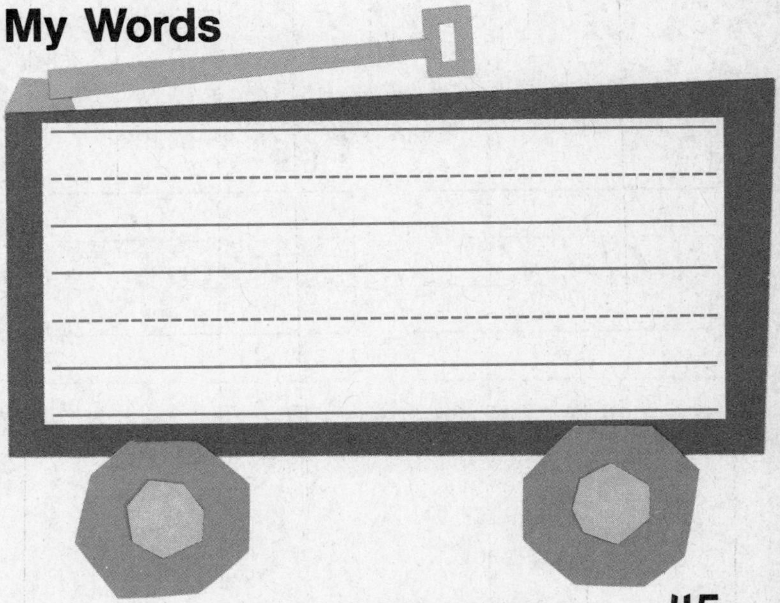

Children trace and write the letter **l** and the words **leaf** and **fall**.

t

tent

telescope

t t t t

late

late

best

best

My Words

Children trace and write the letter **t** and the words **late** and **best**.

h

hook

hat

h   h   h   h

hat   hall

My Words

Children trace and write the letter **h** and the words **hat** and **hall**.

k

kitchen

key

k　k　k　　　　　　　　k

My Words

bake　cook

bake　*cook*

Children trace and write the letter **k** and the words **bake** and **cook**.

Write each word.

tag

bag

flag

goat

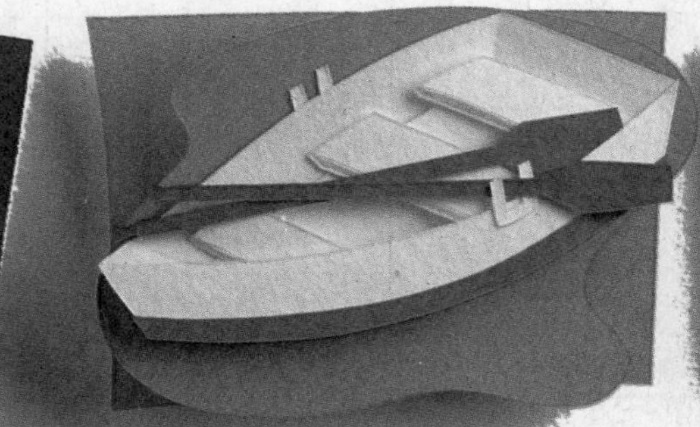

boat

coat

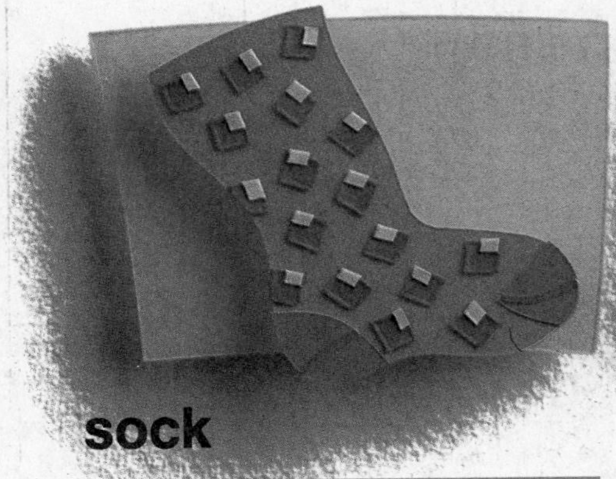

sock

lock

clock

Children write words without a handwriting model.

Practice

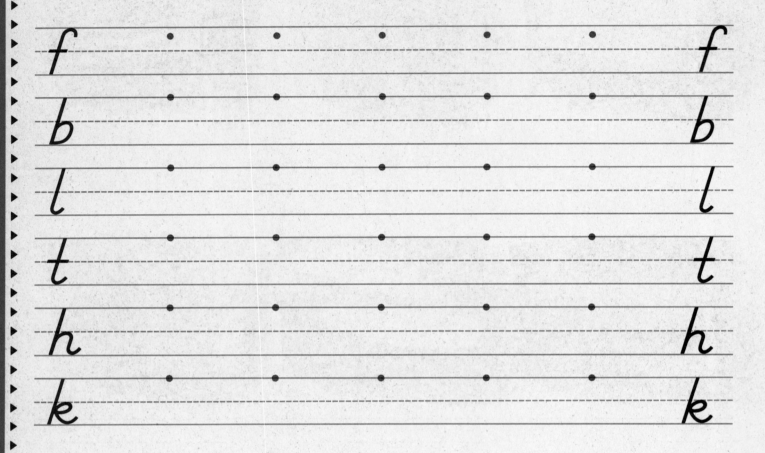

f   f

b   b

l   l

t   t

h   h

k   k

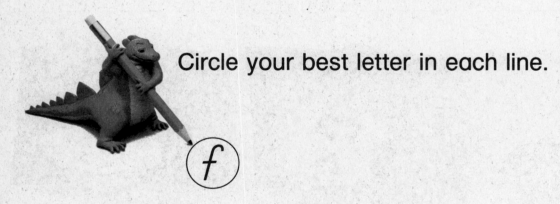

Circle your best letter in each line.

Children write the letters f, b, l, t, h, and k.

Review

basket

basket

cheese

cheese

bat

bat

ball

ball

flags

flags

badge

badge

socks

socks

hat

hat

Children trace and write words with the letters **f**, **b**, **l**, **t**, **h**, and **k**.

Evaluation

Remember: Cross the letters **f** and **t**.

look

look

hot

hot

fast softball

fast softball

a baseball bat

a baseball bat

Check Your Handwriting
Did you cross the letters **f** and **t**?

Yes No
☐   ☐

Children trace and write words and
phrases with the letters **f, b, l, t, h,** and **k**.

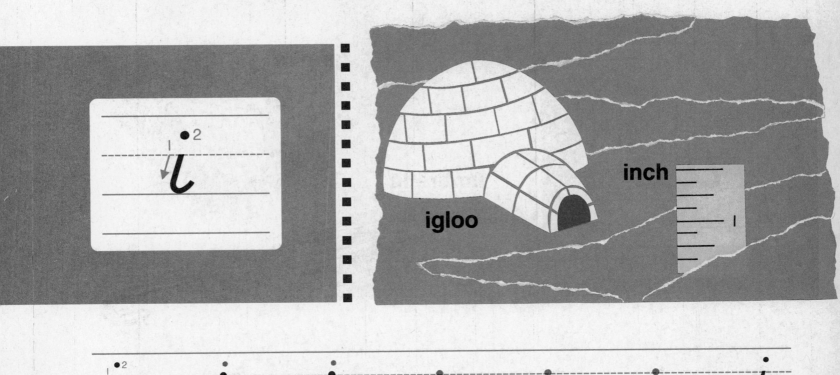

i *i* *i*   *i*

igloo

igloo

My Words

Children trace and write the letter **i** and the word **igloo**.

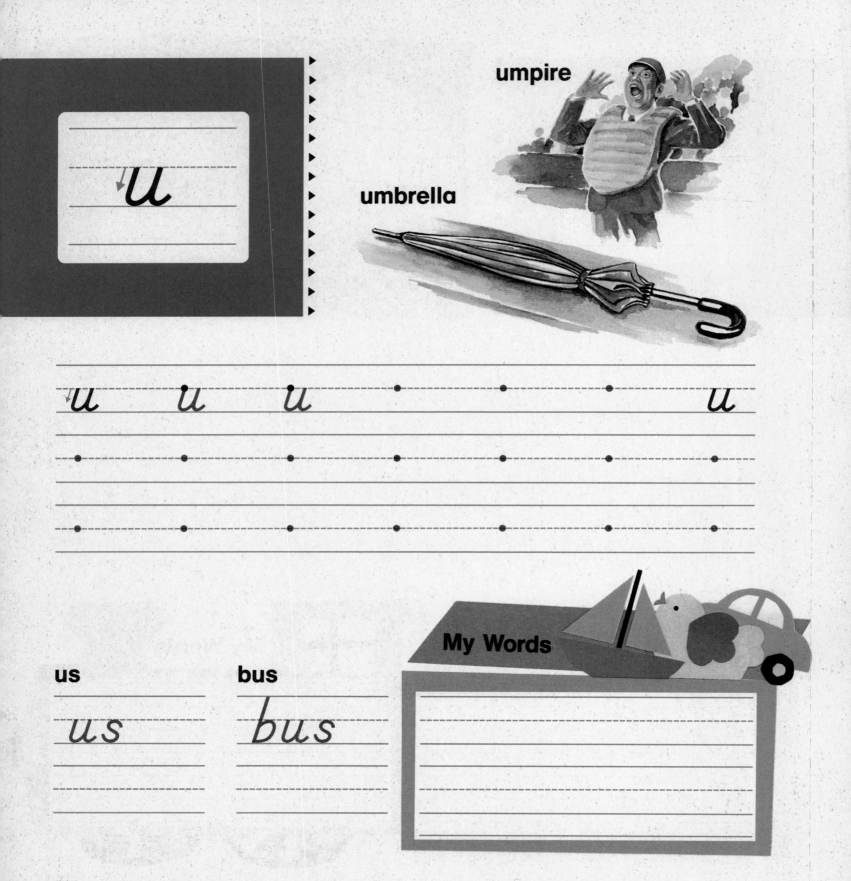

umpire

umbrella

u

u *u* *u* *u*

us

us

bus

bus

My Words

Children trace and write the letter **u** and the words **us** and **bus**.

w

web

wall

w w w · · · w

My Words

web

web

wall

wall

Children trace and write the letter **w** and the words **web** and **wall**.

y

yard

yarn

y   y   y   y

My Words

yellow

yellow

Children trace and write the letter **y** and the word **yellow**.

jack-in-the-box

jet

j

j *j* *j* *j*

jet

jet

joy

joy

My Words

Children trace and write the letter **j** and the words **jet** and **joy**.

r

rabbit   **rock**

r   r   r   r

rabbit

rabbit

My Words

Children trace and write the letter **r** and the word **rabbit**.

nightingales

nest

n   n   n   n   •   •   •   n

My Words

nest   sing

nest   *sing*

Children trace and write the letter **n** and the words **nest** and **sing**.

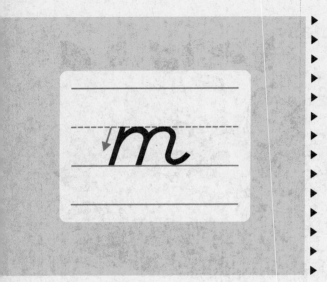

moon

mountain

m   m   m   m

My Words

moon

moon

Children trace and write the letter **m** and the word **moon**.

p

puppet

paper

p

puppet

puppet

My Words

Writing **p** **61**

Children trace and write the letter **p** and the word **puppet**.

Practice

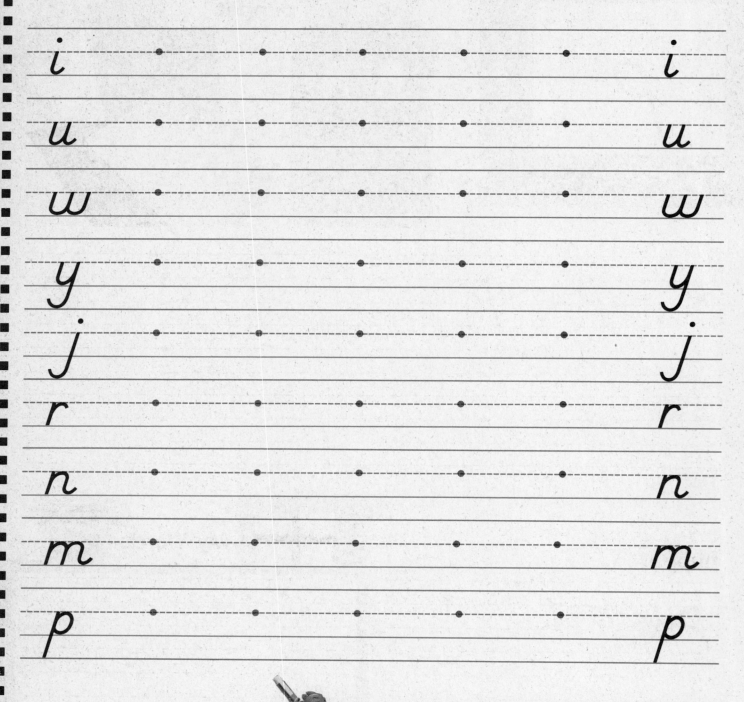

i   i

u   u

w   w

y   y

j   j

r   r

n   n

m   m

p   p

Circle your best letter in each line.

Children write the letters **i, u, w, y, j, r, n, m,** and **p.**

Review

cup

cup

jar

jar

bowl

bowl

milk

milk

kitchen

kitchen

strawberry

strawberry

Children trace and write words with the letters **i, u, w, y, j, r, n, m,** and **p.**

Evaluation

home

home

juice

juice

Remember: Dot the letters **i** and **j**.

birthday party

birthday party

a few friends

a few friends

Check Your Handwriting
Did you dot the letters **i** and **j**?

Yes No
☐   ☐

Children trace and write words and phrases
with the letters **i, u, w, y, j, r, n, m,** and **p.**

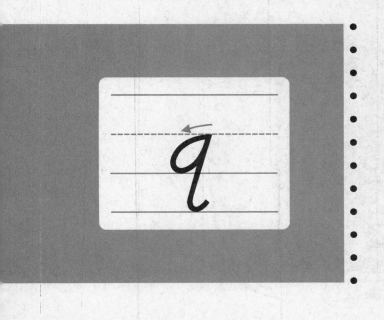

queen

quarter

q q q q q

quarter

quarter

My Words

Children trace and write the letter **q** and the word **quarter.**

valentine

violets

My Words

valentine

valentine

Children trace and write the letter **v** and the word **valentine**.

Z

zebra

Z z z • • • Z

zebra

zebra

My Words

Children trace and write the letter **z** and the word **zebra**.

x ray

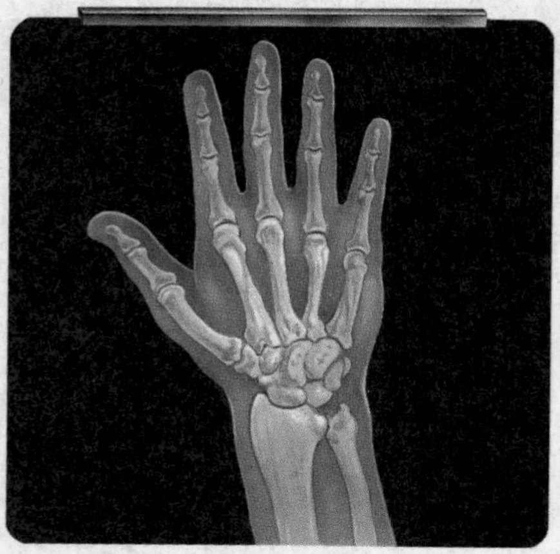

x ray

My Words

x ray

x ray

Children trace and write the letter **x** and the word **x ray**.

Each pair of words makes a new word.
Write each new word.

door   bell

doorbell

_____

- - - - - - - - - - - - - - - - -

_____

mail   box

mailbox

_____

- - - - - - - - - - - - - - - - -

_____

bird   house

birdhouse

_____

- - - - - - - - - - - - - - - - -

_____

fish   net

fishnet

_____

- - - - - - - - - - - - - - - - -

_____

hair   cut

haircut

_____

- - - - - - - - - - - - - - - - -

_____

Children write words without a handwriting model.

Practice

q   q

q   q

v   v

v   v

z   z

z   z

x   x

x   x

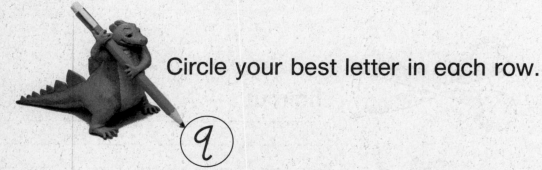

Circle your best letter in each row.

q

Children write the letters **q**, **v**, **z**, and **x**.

Review

ox

ox

fox

fox

quail

quail

zebra

zebra

beaver

beaver

lizard

lizard

Children trace and write words with the letters **q**, **v**, **z**, and **x**.

Evaluation

Remember: Slant all letters the same way.

zoo

zoo

view

view

six animals

six animals

a quiet bear

a quiet bear

Check Your Handwriting
Do all your letters slant the same way?

Yes   No

☐   ☐

Children trace and write words and phrases with the letters **q, v, z,** and **x.**

Reading and Writing

"Pardon?" Said the Giraffe is a funny story.
It is about a **small** frog and a **tall** giraffe.

Look at the picture. Read the sentences.
Find out what the frog wants to know.

"Pardon?"
said the
giraffe.

"What's it like up there?"
asked the frog
as he hopped on the ground.

Can the frog see what the giraffe can see?
Can the giraffe see what the frog can see?
Why do you suppose the giraffe said, "Pardon?"

Writing in Response to Literature   **73**

Imagine you are up high in a tall building.
Pretend you are looking down from a window.
Talk about what things look like on the ground.

Gay saw many things from her apartment window.
Read the sentences Gay wrote about them.

I see little cars.
They crawl like ants.
The trucks look like
big boxes on wheels.
I feel like a giant!

Look at what Gay wrote.

	Yes	No
• Did Gay use describing words?	☐	☐
• Do her sentences make sense?	☐	☐

Look at how she wrote it.

	Yes	No
• Do all her tall letters touch the top line?	☐	☐
• Do all her small letters touch the middle line?	☐	☐
• Do the letters **g** and **y** fall below the line?	☐	☐

What letters are not the correct size?
Circle them.

Children read and evaluate a sample draft.

Now you can write on your own.
Pretend you are in a high place.
What do things look like on the ground?
Write about some things you talked about in class.

_____

- -

_____

- -

_____

- -

_____

- -

_____

- -

_____

Look at what you wrote.   Yes   No
- Did you use good describing words?   ☐   ☐
- Do your sentences make sense?   ☐   ☐

Look at how you wrote it.
- Do all your tall letters touch the top line?   ☐   ☐
- Do all your small letters touch the middle line?   ☐   ☐
- Do your letters **g, j, p, q,** and **y** fall below
  the line?   ☐   ☐

Make any changes that are needed.
Then copy the sentences on your own paper.

Children write sentences about a topic. Then they
revise their sentences and check their handwriting.

The a b c's are not hard to do.
Just say the letters and write them too.

a   b   c

d   e   f

g   h   i   j

k   l   m   n

o   p   q   r

s   t   u   v

w   x   y   z

Children trace and write each lower-case letter of the alphabet.

Name _____

Unit Three
Writing Numbers and Number Words

Trace and write.

1 1 1 1   *one*

one

2 2 2 2   *two*

two

3 3 3 3   *three*

three

78   Writing **1, 2, 3, one, two, three**

Children trace and write the numbers **1, 2,** and **3** and the words **one, two,** and **three.**

Trace and write.

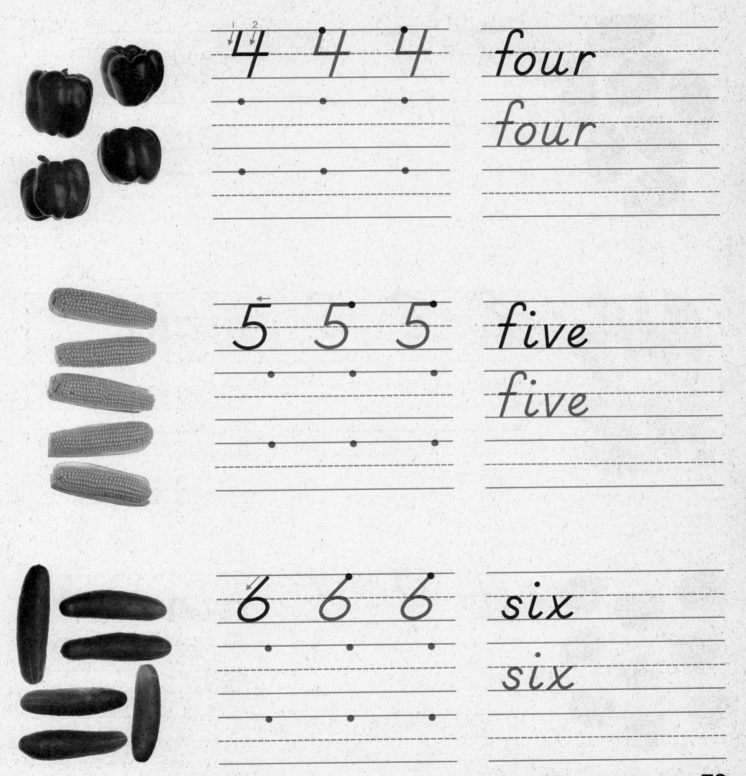

4 4 4   *four*
                 four

5 5 5   *five*
                 five

6 6 6   *six*
                 six

Children trace and write the numbers **4, 5,** and **6** and the words **four, five,** and **six**.

Trace and write.

7 7 7   *seven*

seven

8 8 8   *eight*

eight

9 9 9   *nine*

nine

80 Writing **7, 8, 9, seven, eight, nine**
Children trace and write the numbers **7, 8,**
and **9** and the words **seven, eight,** and **nine.**

Trace and write.

10   10   *ten*

10   *ten*

11   11   *eleven*

11   *eleven*

12   12   *twelve*

12   *twelve*

Children trace and write the numbers **10, 11,**
and **12** and the words **ten, eleven,** and **twelve**.

Practice

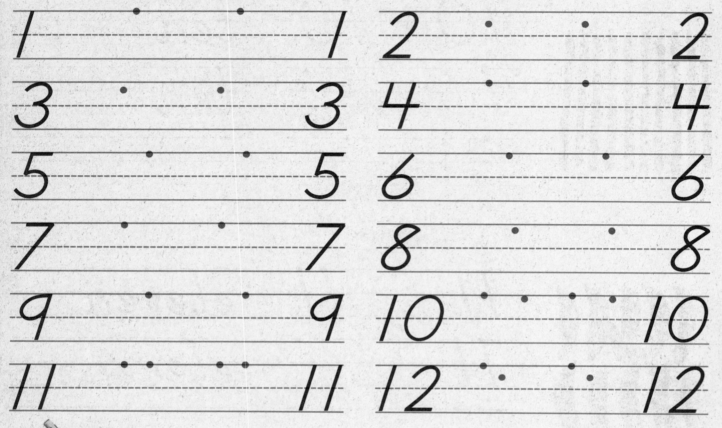

1 ————————————— 1   2 · · · ————— 2
3 · · ————————— 3   4 · · ————————— 4
5 · · ————————— 5   6 · · ————————— 6
7 · · ————————— 7   8 · · ————————— 8
9 · · ————————— 9   10 · · · ——— 10
11 · · · · ——— 11   12 · · · ——— 12

Circle your best number in each line.

Write the numbers **1, 2, 3, 4, 5,** and **6.**

_____

- -

_____

Write the numbers **7, 8, 9, 10, 11,** and **12.**

_____

_____

_____

Children write the numbers 1 through 12.

Review

one

one

l

1

two

two

2

2

three

three

3

3

four

four

4

4

five

five

5

5

six

six

6

6

seven

seven

7

7

eight

eight

8

8

Review **83**

Children trace and write the words **one**
through **eight** and the numbers **l** through **8**.

Evaluation

淑美鮮菜

Remember: Close the numbers **9** and **0**.

nine	9	ten	10
nine	*9*	*ten*	*10*

eleven	11	twelve	12
eleven	*11*	*twelve*	*12*

Check Your Handwriting   Yes   No

Did you close the numbers **9** and **0**?   ☐   ☐

Children trace and write the words **nine** through
twelve and the numbers **9** through **12**.

Name

Unit Four
Writing Capital Letters

There are many ways to write capital letters.
Circle each **F** and **f.**
Draw a line under each **T** and **t.**
Draw a box around each **S** and **s.**
Now draw a path from the house to the school.

Fine Foods

Trash

U. S.
Mail

Bus
Stop

Ash Street

Gas
for
Sale

Stop

Fox School

Children compare the same letters in different type styles. Then they circle
each **F** and **f**, underline each **T** and **t**, and draw a box around each **S** and **s.**

Write all the tall letters.

b d f h k l t

All the capital letters are tall letters too.

A B C D E F G H I
J K L M N O P Q R
S T U V W X Y Z

Write all the small letters.

a c e i m n o r s u v w x z

Write all the letters that fall.

g j p q y

Children write the tall letters, the small letters, and the
descender letters. Then they name the capital letters.

Name all the letters in each group.

Tall Letters

b d f h k l t
A B C D E F G
H I J K L M N
O P Q R S T
U V W X Y Z

Small Letters

a c e i m n o
r s u v w x z

Letters That Fall

g j p q y

Draw a line under the tall letters.
Circle the small letters.
Draw a box around the letters that fall.

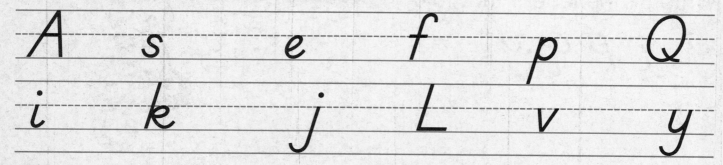

A s e f p Q
i k j L v y

88 Letter Size and Form

Children distinguish different letter sizes. Then they underline the tall letters,
circle the small letters, and draw a box around the descender letters.

All your letters should slant the same way.
You can slant your letters three ways.

straight up and down

Big Top

to the right

Big Top

to the left

Big Top

Read the words.
Circle the words that have the correct slant.

Circus Town

Lions and tigers

dancing bears

Jojo Clown

Children circle the words that show all
the letters slanted in the same direction.

You need to space letters and words.

Do not write letters in a word
too close together.

The band cannot play.

Do not write letters in a word
too far apart.

The band ca

Leave more space between words.

The band can play.

Now write these words.
Ask a friend to read the words.

a marching song

Children compare correct and incorrect letter and word
spacing. Then they write a phrase using correct spacing.

Every letter has a capital and lower-case form.

Aa Bb Cc Dd Ee Ff Gg

Hh Ii Jj Kk Ll Mm

Nn Oo Pp Qq Rr Ss Tt

Uu Vv Ww Xx Yy Zz

Read the riddles. Write the answers.
Use lower-case letters.

What fish shines like a star?
Ss Tt Aa Rr Ff Ii Ss Hh

_____

What fish says meow?
Cc Aa Tt Ff Ii Ss Hh

_____

What fish is very rich?
Gg Oo Ll Dd Ff Ii Ss Hh

_____

Letter Comparison   **91**

Children compare capital and lower-case letters of the alphabet.
Then they write responses to riddles using the lower-case alphabet.

Read the rhyme.
Circle these marks.

? . ' ,

Draw a line under the capital letters.

A Wise Old Owl

A wise old owl lived in an oak ,

The more he saw the less he spoke .

The less he spoke the more he heard .

Why can ' t we all be like that wise old bird ?

Trace and write.

? ? ?

, , ,

Now read the rhyme again.
Put these marks in the correct place.

? . ' ,

A Wise Old Owl

A wise old owl lived in an oak ☐

The more he saw the less he spoke ☐

The less he spoke the more he heard ☐

Why can ☐ t we all be like that wise old bird ☐

92 Punctuation

Children identify, trace, and write question marks, periods, apostrophes, and commas. Then they write punctuation marks to complete sentences in a rhyme.

Cousin Cora

cup

C C C C C C

Cora liked the soup.

Cora liked the soup.

Children trace and write the letter **C** and the sentence **Cora liked the soup**.

Gary Goat

goggles

G G G · · · G

Gary did not feel well.

Gary did not feel well.

Children trace and write the letter **G** and the sentence **Gary did not feel well.**

O

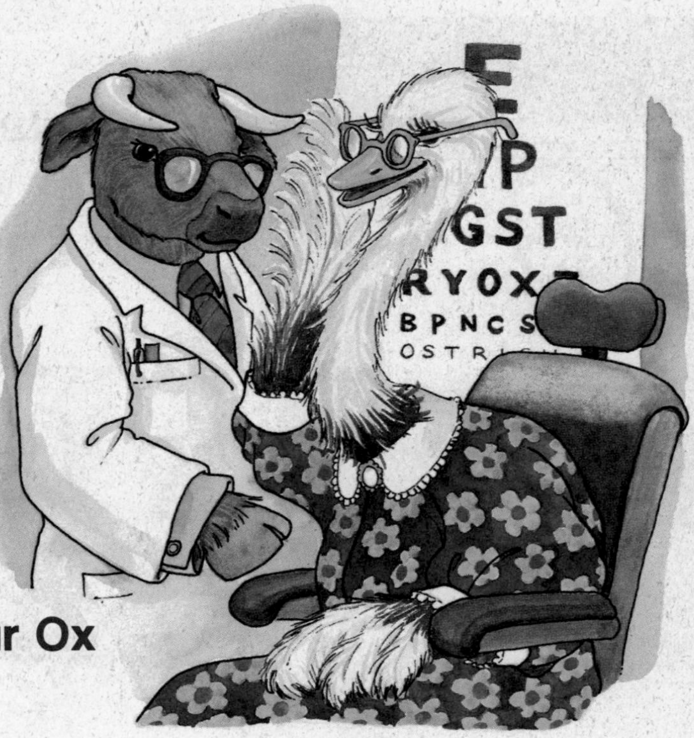

Oscar Ox

ostrich

O O O O

Oscar was glad to help.

Oscar was glad to help.

Children trace and write the letter O and the sentence **Oscar was glad to help.**

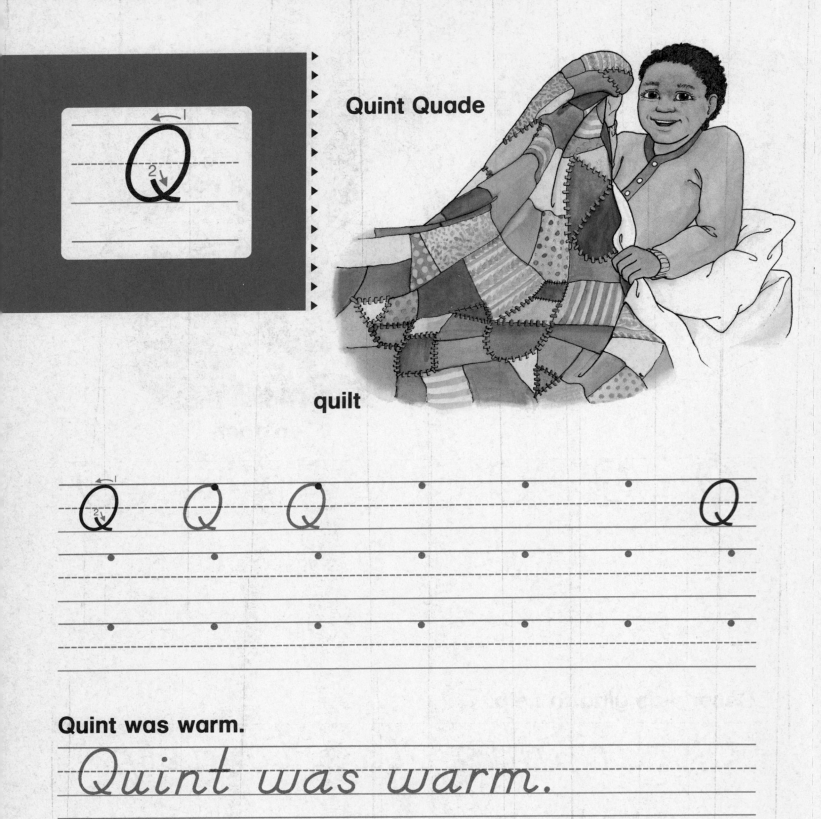

Quint Quade

quilt

Quint was warm.

Quint was warm.

Children trace and write the letter **Q** and the sentence **Quint was warm.**

S

Sumi Seal

sea gulls

S   S   S   .   .   .   S

Sumi sails her boat.

Sumi sails her boat.

Children trace and write the letter **S** and the sentence **Sumi sails her boat.**

Practice

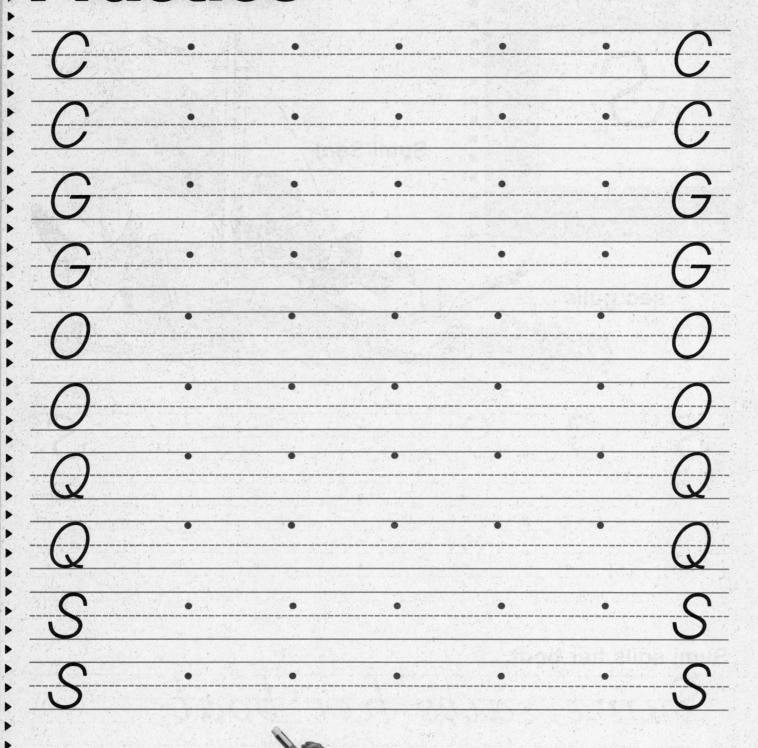

C   •   •   •   •   •   C

C   •   •   •   •   •   C

G   •   •   •   •   •   G

G   •   •   •   •   •   G

O   •   •   •   •   •   O

O   •   •   •   •   •   O

Q   •   •   •   •   •   Q

Q   •   •   •   •   •   Q

S   •   •   •   •   •   S

S   •   •   •   •   •   S

Circle your best letter in each line.

Children write the letters **C**, **G**, **O**, **Q**, and **S**.

Review

Gary

Gary

Oscar

Oscar

Cousin Cora

Cousin Cora

Quint Quade

Quint Quade

Sumi Seal

Sumi Seal

Children trace and write names with the letters **C, G, O, Q,** and **S**.

Evaluation

Doctor Ox

Remember: Curve the letters **C, G, O,** and **S.**

Gary and Sumi are sick.

Gary and Sumi are sick.

Can Oscar help them?

Can Oscar help them?

Check Your Handwriting   Yes No
Did you curve the letters **C, G, O,** and **S?**

☐   ☐

Children trace and write sentences with the letters **C, G, O,** and **S.**

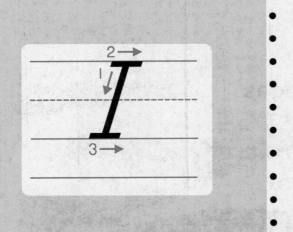

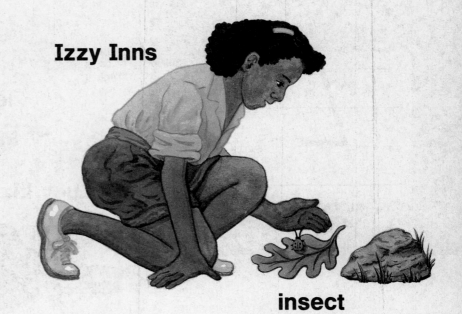

Izzy Inns

insect

I I I I I

Izzy sat on the stone.

Izzy sat on the stone.

Children trace and write the letter I and the sentence **Izzy sat on the stone.**

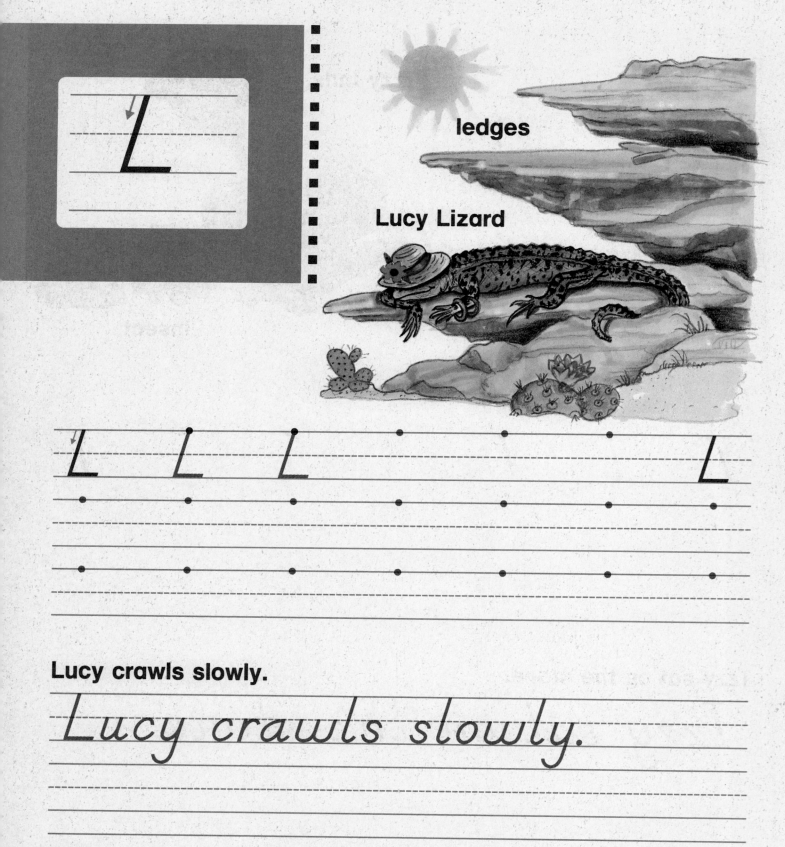

ledges

Lucy Lizard

Lucy crawls slowly.

Lucy crawls slowly.

Children trace and write the letter **L** and the sentence **Lucy crawls slowly.**

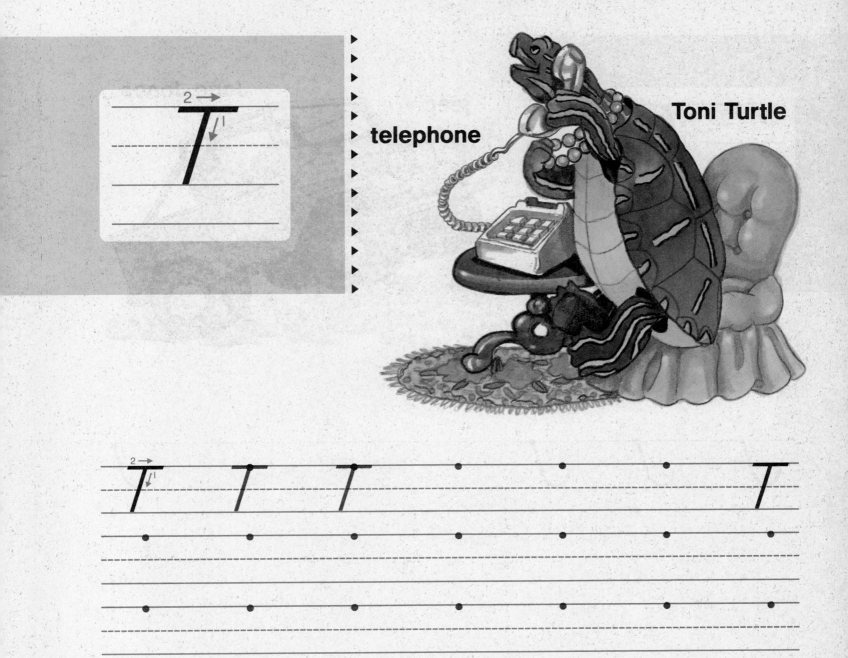

telephone

Toni Turtle

Toni talked for an hour.

Toni talked for an hour.

Children trace and write the letter **T** and the sentence **Toni talked for an hour.**

jeep

Jane Jones

Jane drives safely.

Jane drives safely.

Children trace and write the letter **J** and the sentence **Jane drives safely.**

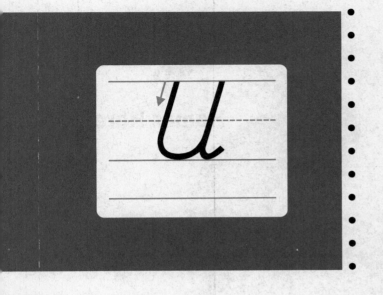

usher

Uncle Ud

U U U   *U*

Uncle Ud saw a show.

Uncle Ud saw a show.

Children trace and write the letter **U** and the sentence **Uncle Ud saw a show.**

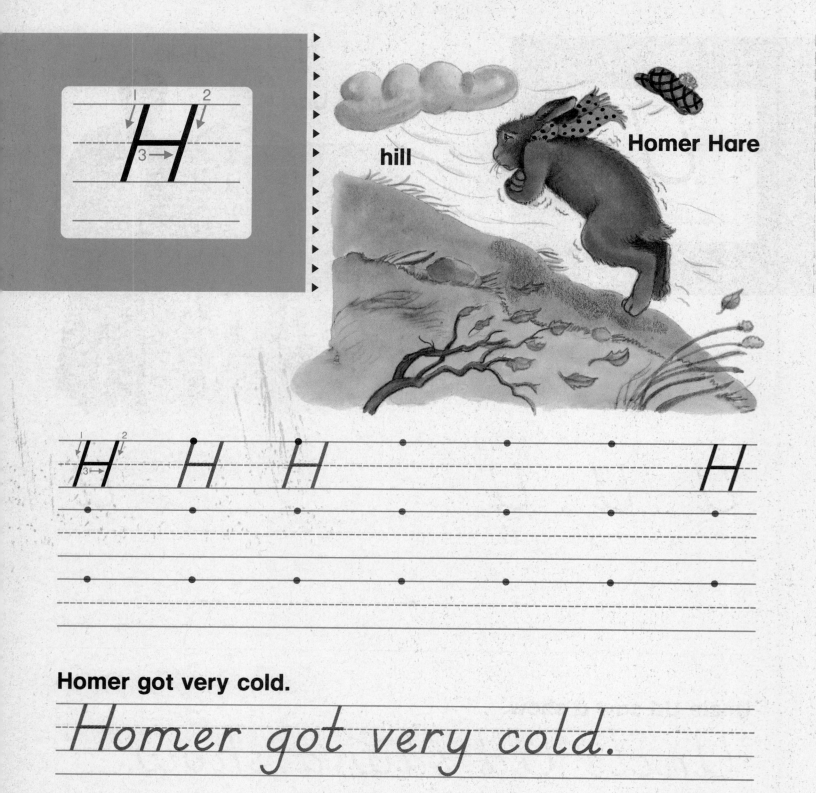

hill

Homer Hare

Homer got very cold.

Homer got very cold.

Children trace and write the letter **H** and the sentence **Homer got very cold.**

Kang Koo

kite

K K K   K

Kang makes his kite.

Kang makes his kite.

Children trace and write the letter **K** and the sentence **Kang makes his kite.**

Practice

I   I

L   L

T   T

J   J

U   U

H   H

K   K

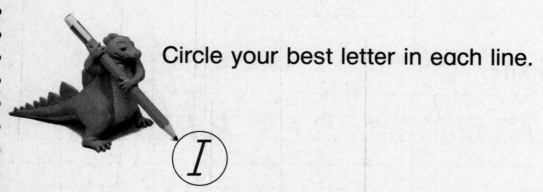

Circle your best letter in each line.

Children write the letters **I, L, T, J, U, H,** and **K.**

Review

Izzy

Izzy

Lucy

Lucy

Toni

Toni

Jane

Jane

Homer

Homer

Kang

Kang

Uncle Ud

Uncle Ud

Children trace and write names with the letters **I, L, T, J, U, H,** and **K.**

Evaluation

Remember: The letters **I** and **T** have crossbars.

Jane gave Izzy a ride.

Jane gave Izzy a ride.

They invited Kang.

They invited Kang.

Check Your Handwriting
Did you remember the crossbars
for **I** and **T**?

Yes No

☐   ☐

Children trace and write sentences with the letters **I, T, J,** and **K.**

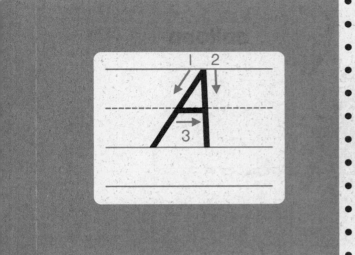

Anna Alligator

ambulance

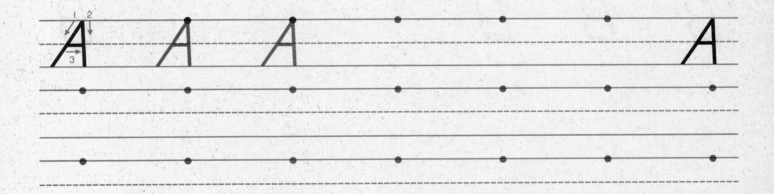

Anna is much better.

Anna is much better.

Children trace and write the letter **A** and the sentence **Anna is much better.**

balloon

Becky Belle

B *B* *B* *B*

Becky lost her balloon.

Becky lost her balloon.

Children trace and write the letter **B** and the sentence **Becky lost her balloon**.

D

Don Diaz

dinosaur

D D D · · · · · D

Don was a lucky boy.

Don was a lucky boy.

Children trace and write the letter **D** and the sentence **Don was a lucky boy.**

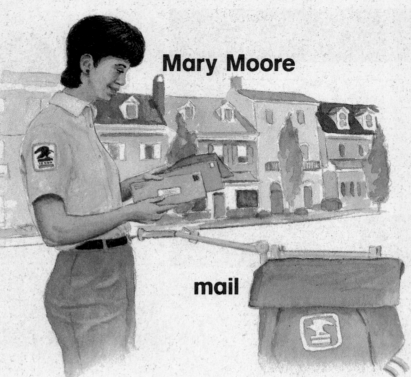

Mary Moore

mail

M M M M   M

Mary does a good job.

Mary does a good job.

Children trace and write the letter **M** and the sentence **Mary does a good job**.

Nicky Norton

newspaper

Nicky read for a while.

Nicky read for a while.

Children trace and write the letter **N** and the sentence **Nicky read for a while.**

picture

Paula Panda

P

P P P   P

Paula painted well.

Paula painted well.

Children trace and write the letter **P** and the sentence **Paula painted well.**

R

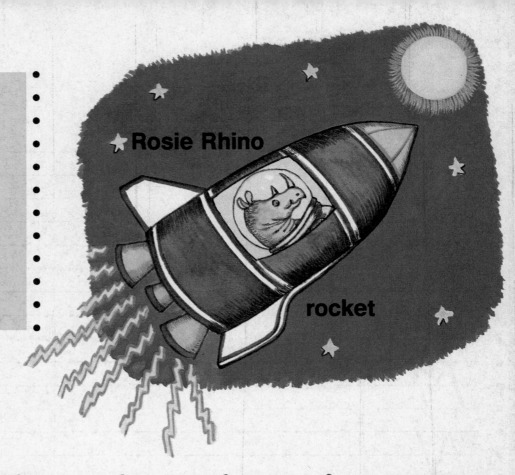

Rosie Rhino

rocket

R R R   *R*

Rosie zoomed away fast.

Rosie zoomed away fast.

Children trace and write the letter **R** and the sentence **Rosie zoomed away fast.**

Practice

A   A

B   B

D   D

M   M

N   N

P   P

R   R

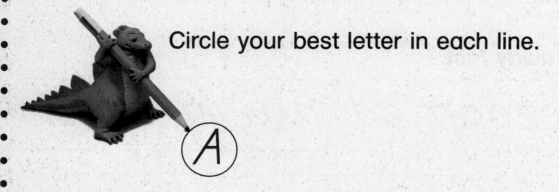

Circle your best letter in each line.

Ⓐ

Children write the letters **A, B, D, M, N, P,** and **R.**

Review

Anna

Anna

Don

Don

Becky

Becky

Mary

Mary

Nicky

Nicky

Paula

Paula

Rosie Rhino

Rosie Rhino

Children trace and write names with
the letters **A, B, D, M, N, P,** and **R.**

Evaluation

Remember: Close the letters **D**, **P**, and **R**.

Does Paula have paints?

Does Paula have paints?

Anna and Rosie smile.

Anna and Rosie smile.

Check Your Handwriting

Did you close the letters **D**, **P**, and **R**?

Yes No

☐ ☐

Children trace and write sentences with the letters **A**, **D**, **P**, and **R**.

escalator

Eddie Elf

E E E E

Eddie liked to ride.

Eddie liked to ride.

Children trace and write the letter **E** and the sentence **Eddie liked to ride.**

Fay Fine **farm**

F F F F · · · · F

Fay gets up early.

Fay gets up early.

Children trace and write the letter **F** and the sentence **Fay gets up early.**

Z

zipper

Zack Zole

Z Z Z Z

Zack fixed his jacket.

Zack fixed his jacket.

Writing **Z**   **123**

Children trace and write the letter **Z** and the sentence **Zack fixed his jacket.**

Vi Vega

violin

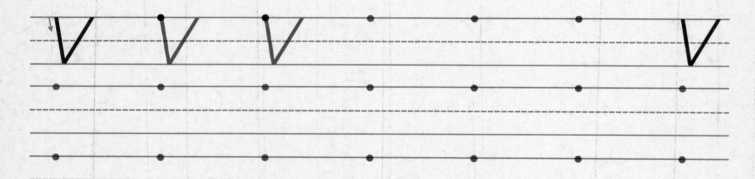

Vi plays nice tunes.

Vi plays nice tunes.

Children trace and write the letter **V** and the sentence **Vi plays nice tunes.**

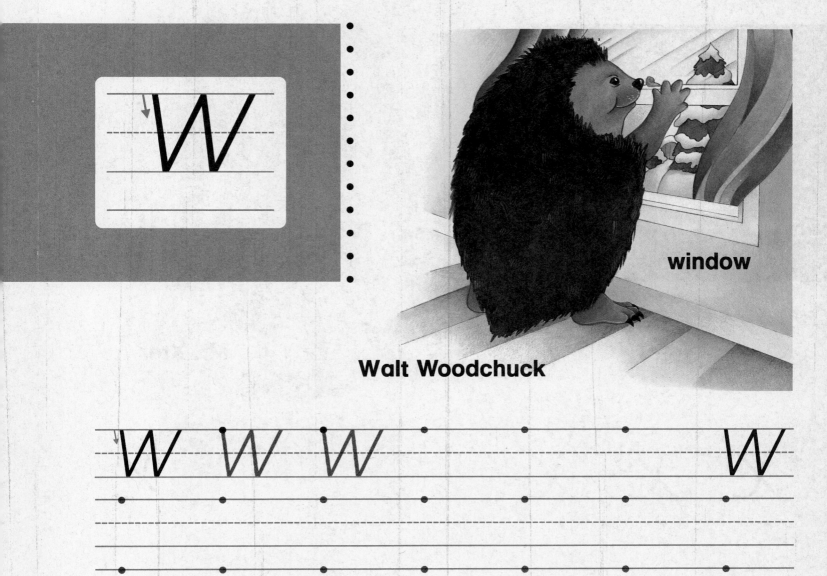

window

Walt Woodchuck

W W W   W

Walt found his drapes.

Walt found his drapes.

Children trace and write the letter **W** and the sentence **Walt found his drapes.**

Mr. Xter

X X X · · · · X

Mr. Xter is an acrobat.

Mr. Xter is an acrobat.

Children trace and write the letter **X** and the sentence **Mr. Xter is an acrobat**.

Yelda Yak

yams

Yelda eats her treats.

Yelda eats her treats.

Children trace and write the letter **Y** and the sentence **Yelda eats her treats.**

Practice

E   E

F   F

Z   Z

V   V

W   W

X   X

Y   Y

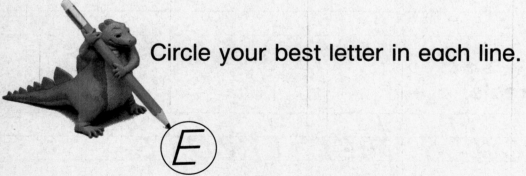

Circle your best letter in each line.

E

Children write the letters **E, F, Z, V, W, X,** and **Y**.

Review

Eddie

Eddie

Fay

Fay

Zack

Zack

Vi

Vi

Walt

Walt

Yelda

Yelda

Mr. Xter

Mr. Xter

Children trace and write names with the letters **E, F, Z, V, W, X,** and **Y.**

Evaluation

Remember: Slant all the letters the same way.

Fay and Vi sing.

Fay and Vi sing.

Will Mr. Xter act?

Will Mr. Xter act?

Check Your Handwriting   Yes   No
Do all your letters slant the same way?   ☐   ☐

Children trace and write sentences with the letters **F**, **V**, **W**, and **X**.

A   B   C
D   E   F
G   H   I   J
K   L   M   N
O   P   Q   R
S   T   U   V
W   X   Y   Z

Children write each capital letter of the alphabet.

You need to fill out a form for a library card.
Complete the form.

Library Card

Name _____

Address _____

City _____

You may need to fill out a form for a bus pass.
Complete the form.

Bus Pass

Name _____

School _____

Children complete forms for a library card and a bus pass.

There are seven days in a week.
Read the names in the correct order.

1. Sunday   2. Monday   3. Tuesday

4. Wednesday   5. Thursday   6. Friday   7. Saturday

Trace and write the names.

Sunday

Monday

Tuesday

Wednesday

Children trace and write the first four days of the week.

Thursday

Friday

Saturday

Pick your favorite day of the week.
What do you like to do?
Draw a picture.

Children trace and write the last three days of the week. Then they draw a picture of their favorite activity for a specific day.

There are twelve months in the year.
Read the names in the correct order.

January

February

March

April

May

June

July

August

September

October

November

December

Trace and write the months.

January

February

March

April

Children trace and write the names of the first four months of the year.

May

June

July

August

September

October

November

December

136 Writing Months of the Year

Children trace and write the names of the last eight months of the year.

Sonia invited Laura to a party.
Read Sonia's invitation.

To: *Laura*

What: *Sleep-over Party*

When: *Friday at 6:00 P.M.*

Where: *27 Long Street*

From: *Sonia*

Copy the invitation on your own paper.
Don't forget to close the letters **a, d, o**, and **g.**

Children copy an invitation.

Laura wrote Sonia to thank her for her party.
Read Laura's thank-you note.

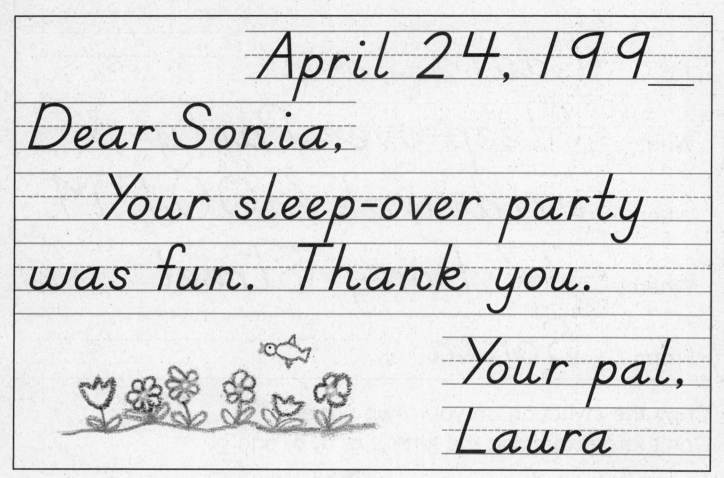

April 24, 199__

Dear Sonia,
*   Your sleep-over party*
was fun. Thank you.

*   Your pal,*
Laura

Copy the thank-you note on your own paper.
Remember to slant your letters the same way.

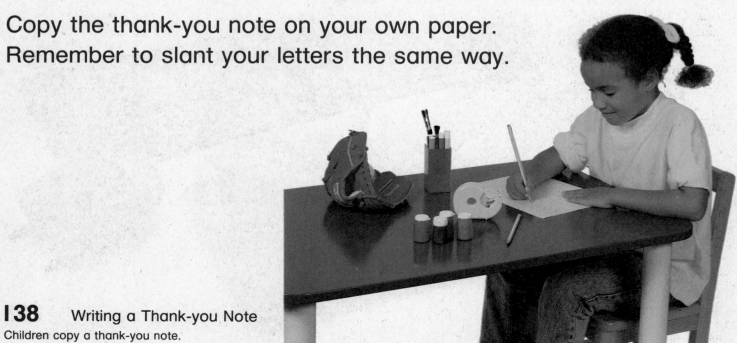

Children copy a thank-you note.

Read the directions for making a bookmark.

1. Get paper and crayons.
2. Draw a pet you like.
3. Write your name on the bookmark.
4. Cut it out carefully.
5. Put it inside a book.

Copy the directions on your own paper.
Leave more space between words than letters.

Now follow the directions. Make a bookmark.

1.

2.

3.

4.

5.

Children copy a set of directions for making a bookmark.
Then they use the directions to make their own bookmarks.

Read the joke. Then copy it.
Remember to use capital letters.
Don't forget to use these marks.

| ? | . | ' | , |

Jim, where's your dog?
I don't know.
Do you give up?
Yes, I do.
It's in a barking lot.

_____
- -
_____
- -
_____
- -
_____
- -
_____
- -
_____

Children copy a joke without a handwriting model.

Reading and Writing

Eat Up, Gemma is a funny story. Gemma is a baby who won't eat until she finds something that makes eating fun to do.

Look at the picture. Read the sentences. Find out what makes Gemma want to eat.

When everyone was really quiet Gemma leaned forward.
"Eat up, Gemma," she said.
Then she tried to pull a grape off the lady's hat. She pulled and pulled and the lady's hat fell off. Gemma hid her face in Dad's coat. ■

Writing in Response to Literature **141**

Children read sentences from a book.

Think back to the time when you were little.
Draw a picture about something funny you did.

Carlos wrote a story about when he was little.
Read the sentences he wrote to tell about it.

I put on my d a d ' s hat,
his c o a t, and his shoes.
Then I looked in the
m i r r o r and saw my
dad's face l o o k i n g at me!

Look at what Carlos wrote.   Yes No
- Are his sentences in the correct order?   ☐   ☐
- Did he have a good ending to his story?   ☐   ☐

Look at how he wrote it.
- Is there the same amount of space between
  all the letters in his words?   ☐   ☐
- Is there more space between his words than
  between his letters?   ☐   ☐

What letters and words do not have the
correct spacing? Circle them.

Children read and evaluate a sample draft.

Now you can write your own funny story.
Use your picture to help you think of some ideas.

_____

_____

_____

_____

_____

_____

_____

_____

_____

_____

_____

Look at what you wrote.   Yes   No
- Are your sentences in the correct order?   ☐   ☐
- Do you have a good ending to your story?   ☐   ☐

Look at how you wrote it.
- Is there the same amount of space between
  all the letters in your words?   ☐   ☐
- Is there more space between your words than
  between your letters?   ☐   ☐

Make any changes that are needed. Then copy
the sentences on your own paper.

Children write a story. Then they revise their
sentences and check their handwriting.

Index